journey into fulfillment

Journey into Fulfillment

by M. J. Scott

A Hearthstone Book

Carlton Press, Inc.   New York, N.Y.

© Copyright 1972 by M.J. Scott
ALL RIGHTS RESERVED
Manufactured in the United States of America

Dedicated to my husband and daughters — for their gift of moments given when "quiet and peace" could meet in the Master's Presence, and for their continuing encouragement so that JOURNEY INTO FULFILLMENT can now belong to you.

                                                        M.J. Scott

CONTENTS

I. JOURNEY'S BEGINNING THOUGHTS	13
There Is a Day	13
Who?	14
Hello Journey	15
Ignition Switch	17
II. PERSONAL BELONGINGS	19
Degree of Happiness	19
Traveling Into Self	20
Stop Dreaming!	21
Why Frustration	22
III. AWAKENING TO AWARENESS	24
Autumn Notes	24
Responsive Meaning	24
Winged Experiences	25
Country Kitchen	27
Fingers of Fog	28
Six o'Clock Chimes	29
Edge of Decision	30
Chiffon Effect	31
IV INNER TRACES OF URGING	33
Heart's Concerto	33
Art of the Concerned	34
Circlets of Inspiration	34
Half-Time	35
The Natural Effect	36
One-Half a Pair	37

V.	THE PHYSICAL REMINDERS OF VALUE	40
	A Package of Attic Thoughts	40
	Tranquility Base	41
	That Which Is Within	41
	Instead	42
VI.	MENTAL INTO SPIRIT RETURN	44
	Experimenting With Expression	44
	Serenade of Christmas Thoughts	45
	The Long Dry Spell	46
	Video Mind	47
	Full Measure of Satisfaction	48
	Turn Ahead	49
VII	THE HIGH ROAD	51
	Blank For Beginning	51
	Journey's Throne	52
	The Filtering Silence	53
	Altar of Encounter	54
	Praise To Lift	55
	The Perfect Signature	55
	Contentment's Form	56
	Try To Retire	57
	Entering In	58
	The Great Quest!	59
	God's Meaning and Author's Inspiration	61

PROLOGUE

This title begins a long journey that was realized not at the onset but later after many miles of type had rolled beneath the keys. The moment of realization began upon a wintertime scene with a great moment of blending search and desire into purpose.

Purpose has carried into manuscripts now written and greater joy in traveling now ahead in sharing new sights with you the reader.

Let it be your own journey into fulfillment with growing awareness to the beauty surrounding each day. Let the travels become your moments of recapturing peace and move the soul with nurturing strength.

The blending of life to build a fine portrait doesn't begin tomorrow with the perfect canvas size and color chart. Each day to live as though the last, brings moments to meaning, experiences into perceptive awareness, and happiness to you and yours.

Welcome aboard, be prepared for detours and reconstruction but greatest of all, finding the route that the Master has helped us to see. Journey Into Fulfillment, the way lies open, and hearts leap to begin.

M.J. Scott

journey into fulfillment

I. JOURNEY'S BEGINNING THOUGHTS

THERE IS A DAY

There is a day when schedules dissolve and appointments for kinks and curls can be rolled into new rhythms. Today it is, when this heart says change, exclaim and find better claims for the time.

Ladies elegant in white gloves, eating morsels of tasty tid-bits surrounding themselves in countries accent of here and there. There's grace and beauty of their fine countenances, but today is dressed in Indian summer glory and burnished with hazel locks and bittersweet berries. Her gloves and dress waltz to the breezes and forever this heart can't cancel this love for Autumn.

Thus there is a day to sing and greet, another day to eat the luncheons of faraway countries best of taste, but today, not today! The music spilling throughout this old mansion lets it live again and this heart loves its inspiring old beauty, on this date with today, and yesterday living together, but for a golden sundrop.

Paintings surround museums and in the word you'll find two u's. Could it be for you to find this creative stroke within your own reach? Could it be your expression of fingertips, brush and paint to become reality, on there is a day of real release? Have you ever tried anymore than to laugh at the thought? Up, up and away the talent drops with the thought and put away in a neat filing drawer of the mind. Lock up all those precious personal thoughts — no one will know you have a talent stored! No auctioneer could find its price, no collector find its hiding place.

Or is there music bound up within your vocal chords? Those can stay close to the heart and unexercised too. Who dares to ask these questions of you? Who knows you as well as God who created you within His Own Heart and Mind? He's awaiting great expression of your latent talents, while you scoff at them with more vigor than the creative effort would require. Why do you say, "I wished I were somewhere else today?" Would you really do any better with the day than make more vain wishes?

Ladies and gentlemen in the court of life — your address may be a status marker, or your title the status symbol, but what do you give each day to make this once upon life special?

"Happiness!" "There Is A Day!" Are these all titles upon chapters of your life unwritten? Are you so busy reading the lives of others to realize greater impact you have within your own witness? Where are you going? The music races the valleys, plains, mountains and sky, and my heart keeps the pace though steps could never comply. So places to fly we'll reach the summit of living, not at tables of conference, but in talks with the Master who is within our very own presence.

Christ knows our hearts, and today He wanted more than a ginger ale for a cocktail, He wanted more than a Canadian feast, He wanted more than a beauty shop set. He wanted the schedule put away, and to realize that "There Is A Day" when happiness sings higher than what walls can contain.

World outside my door at dawn, but at noon world inside my heart has grown into more than "There Is A Day." There is now — for giving so much fragrance to breathing — by looking close and finding our own homes with happiness first. Queen Elizabeth roses, how much the scent reaches the heart in sweetness, beauty and today.

WHO?

"Who-who," says the owl upon an Autumn night.
"Who," says the man upon a midnight dream.
"Who," says the lady to answer the door.
"Who," says the child at lessons to learn.

Who is a word that has tone and question and easily asked. But a small word having difficulty in coming to grips with total understanding. Especially when it reaches inward and comes out, "Who Am I?" Now the "who-who" sound of the owl was the easiest to reckon with his deep eyes and feathery size.

Mankind finds itself in more unique situations than the owl upon the forest night. Owl goes winging in flight for food. Man goes hurrying to work for that same commodity and shelter provider too. After all these are answered, "Who upon man's nightmare refuses to reach answer?"

The lady and child find specific answers, but "Who AM I?" dogs the brain far more than the Social Security number after your name. Man was made to dream and build his dreams into creative purpose. How far has your own journey into fulfillment taken you? Sand castles at the seashore, illusions in powdery clouds disappear, all these are marked by movement and change. How much does man change and mature each day? Who cares asks self?

Yes, more care than you'll ever know. There is Christ to share in this century of growth so rapid. God to guide with His constant protection. Holy Spirit so fragile, yet powerful, can build you into the dynamic Christian that lives and breathes with the good life and hand to encourage those surrounding your life.

Who? Starting out in this journey whatever the map may say, there's more than one crossroad for decision. Who Am I? Where Am I Going? "Just take my hand and guide me," a song that's lilting across lips of youth, beaded in their ways of living yet they are asking for someone to take their hand. Watch and see whose hand they seek.

Who and where? His Hand to Guide!

HELLO JOURNEY

Today has begun with the first journey down the white oyster-crushed lane to the bus stop on the grocery store corner.

Coffee interlude with husband handsome in fresh shirt ironed as dawn cracked up the river. Trip to the office to accompany the white chariot on four unrubbed wheels, yet that is!

Home and today. It's sunny, beautiful, quiet and lots to do, and hours of freedom to begin. The phone breaks the mockingbirds drink beneath the window sill and "yes" breaks convention to be a flower judge at a hymn sing arrangement. That's no record to break when bottom of the barrel is this one to do it. Ah sweet Thursday! The washer is humming her own staccato overture, and the dryer hushed in cycling anticipation. Several new magazines cross paths with progress and feeding the cat. The "Instructor" lures the old warhorse with a nudge but the ties that bind was eyes to see that a right-handed artist made better right-slanted eyes on the cover. Now that's real study to figure out that much about the unseen painter. Between the lines has a mental stimulation of its own accomplishment.

Journey of today how dull some might say. But to those who have careened through a career upon the ticks of a clock, it's sheer ecstasy to stop the hand and find it free.

Husband happy for a flying he will go — today to New York and tonight back home. Children to school and myriad plans to be made. While I mix Halloween, Thanksgiving, Christmas, prefaces, introductions, stories all across a page of happiness. Journey, I love your name and Fulfillment reigning at the beginning and end. Where shall we go today — you and I?

Out to the typewriter to run a Santa Anita winner? Out to the kitchen and cook up a dish for company's frozen future coming? Up to the attic and anticipate when to begin? Down to the cellar and ponder a new invention for leaking water tables? "Up, Up and Away," and off in a cloud of enthusiasm for today we'll go shopping and find material to surprise a birthday box, or wrap a package of happiness in a gift box and label it "tender."

Hello Journey today we shall make a shopping list. WANTED!
1. A lady with a happy face.
2. Mother strolling a baby and watching the ships return.
3. Sun gleaming on the yachts at anchor with light of solitude.
4. Murmur of children's voices happily playing at the school playground.

5. An executive's briefcase swinging on the hand of accomplishment.
6. A motorist who has time for pedestrians to cross unharried at the crosswalk.
7. A butcher out to see a slice of the sun.
8. A baker watching the donuts being conveyed away from the oven.
9. A small hand pressed to a puppy's collar.
10. Three sea gulls flying formation.
11. Ducks winging south and the direction we'd love to go.
12. Postman with letters of happiness for the invalid next door.

Somewhere in one of those is true fulfillment if they only took the time to find the moment open for reflection.

"Hello Journey," you are quite a companion.

IGNITION SWITCH

The insertion of a key into an ignition built for starting, finds turn of a key the promotion of energy. Energy to propel the great vehicle — car, boat or plane — is intricately designed to follow a schematic. Engineers spend time across drawing boards maintaining perfection before that automated object ever made manufacturing dollars.

Thus in reverse we've stopped to think about the intricate means by which the ignition came to be useable. Silence of thought is being scolded in chant, by wild duck's call, to depart his sanctuary here in the estuary. He lunges into the stream and leaves in dismay while waters dance in the tides return.

Ignition to turn can be a mechanical kind, or it can be instinctive as related to the mallard's cry. What makes the minnows leap from surfaces' element? What brings the barnacles to cling to the pier? What switches the winds, and tide, and sand?

Whatever today brings you to find, there's a switch in your thoughts that can change your direction. What births desire for the new? What bears the new into reality? What reality brings life to splendor? What splendor can the eyes contain? What heart can contain it all and share none of this radiant energy? Where did this energy of the human frame devolve? What ignition ignited the form into breath? What form of human dreams has never sensed all higher engineering for his life than this?

What now of today with the ignition in action? Where are you going and why? Close the page, turn off the thought but computers have already found the imprint projected into minds' capacity. Capacity for learning and living come in igniting the great ability into action and deed. Beauty of deed though humbleness dwells beneath the ink, and heart, and soul-sharing is glorious beneath the Master's Eyes.

There's beauty in living just awaiting every Soul. The need and deed must be united like ignition and the key.

Switch on the living with the good life surrounding.

II. PERSONAL BELONGINGS

DEGREE OF HAPPINESS

What degree of happiness are you seeking along this journey of life and its fulfillments?

The important things! Finding yourself and learning to live with this "self" can be a very challenging experience. Not just your name and your physical size for buying clothes, but the inner you and what makes happiness within. Happiness isn't any artificial coloring or substance drank. It's genuine, and knowing what true satisfaction can be. Restlessness is only the stirring within seeking toward satisfaction. Satisfaction is not complacency, it's a degree of inner reward for a degree of worth, attainment and fulfillment.

Degrees marked with a date in time when requirements for scholastic progress was rewarded. Tucked now within its dark leather covering and put away. The degree was achieved, but what about the key to the beginning of learning of life that surrounds and can impound "self"? What degree of happiness are you seeking? Has searching found a tangent and become misplaced?

Upon a morning watching football clothing drying, brings memories of games where self tumbled, fumbled and made the goal. Tablecloths and sheets drying too, the neighbors' use of sunshine and line. Sunshine and step, with pen in hand, finds this time to review how exciting life can be if we but let it BE.

Degree of happiness what is today's contents? Reached upon the final exam, or reached when the score is in? Are people today striving on and on, and hope to find happiness' door at the journey's end?

Happiness must be daily caught, traced with its intricate design and not withheld, but let to move on for others to share. Open your eyes clouded with moss and there comes spring bringing bulbs of promise. Happiness is promised for tomorrow too, for those who live today in its warmth.

Extend it to others, and continue to grow in the light which is daily given for mind and spirit's illumination.

Who, Where and Why? Degree of happiness results in higher interest as the investment is made. Degree of Happiness — how rare your shine!

TRAVELING INTO SELF

Mind travels faster than the motorboats coursing through the Lafayette waves. Thoughts traverse distance and are marked not with punctuation's hesitation.

Journey like the sand, wrestles with movement and so akin to mind. The feeling of reaching out in adventurous search, drills deeper than roots of today's anchor. The cold damp feeling of a brick wall for a seat brings physical awareness and chill. Chill to the bones, as wind through the pines blows too. Great waves beneath the view from that boat's hasty retreat. These physical bits of awareness are mixing with great rushes of destiny's call.

Bombardment of inner desires hammering out their own intricate pattern, and could be even more resounding than the squirrels countless shells away. These little creatures are busy today harvesting nuts for winter's store. Heart is pounding out desire for harvest and more for planting greater dreams toward fulfillment. Hand of the heart is speaking through mind into words that the eyes can see. Interpretation kindles back into mind's recesses, and in joint treaty between mind and heart, Soul finds fruit of discernment and accomplishment.

A brick jostles free, another nut bounces out of the sky. Wind, raises her voice to utterance and waves of the bay wrestle upon the shore. Dreams jostle free, dreams pounce upon the heart, lips raise utterance and man wrestles with life. Living the best, in search of greater mortar of knowledge, while seasons come and go. Mankind so ready to accept each day and give it no freshness, give it no thought. Take what it offers and take no thought. No thought to life is a stagnant dross of existence. Taking life's beauty and adding none in return is parasitic and will eventually destroy even the first seen beauty.

Hello to living above the clouds of uncertainty. Sweep away this darkness with daily walks in the garden of thought, daily thoughts of, "When We Walk With The Lord In The Beauty Of Holiness." Hallowed this day in His Kingdom and realization is the first veil to lift, the candle of thought that will bring light.

STOP DREAMING!

Stop dreaming, and go back to work screams mind at a hurdle between patience and frustration. To stop dreaming is like the coffee pot that was filled with hot water and never perked. That's only a muddied version of living when no dreams are allowed. Dreams begin to focus into goals and are worth all the grains of time in the creating.

Stop dreaming, never! To stop dreaming is to stop believing that greater things are meant to be. Great moments in life were lighted by a tiny sparkling thought that took form, semblance of meaning and became useable.

"Stop," says the sign at the crossing ahead. "Stop," says the crossing guard at the school zone. "Stop," says the light at another intersection. All these stops are for a moment needed to enact motion from another direction. While man is so busy propelling himself along his life's choices, it takes the "stop" to catch up with the man. Here in this fragile instant a new thought can be projected, when man is least suspecting, he is less aware of building resistances to this force.

Resistance is built as a personal insulation to the impact of change upon the life. Life with any uncertainties cause some to shatter in despair, while others find themselves and become like new people from the experience's lesson.

Lesson in living how exciting this day. Determination requires effort, effort and work, mesh into an objective and purpose has been brought to bear by stopping for a "need."

Never stop dreaming, for here in this fragile proving ground is the finest of experiments performed. No test ground rules signed in a treaty pact, it's you that's the projectionist, the engineer, the model and the mold. To stop dreaming is closing the door of creativity, locking it tight with the inhibited fears of no self confidence and signing your own scroll of defeat.

Dreams are built with eyes wide open, ears and heart attuned, and thought plays the triumphal entry march.

WHY FRUSTRATION

"Why," screams the mind tangling in a duel between frustration and patience. "Because," calls the heart, "there must be decision." Decision marks growth, and growth yields toward maturity. Maturity never ceases, and becomes greater, as long as open mindedness is a way of thinking.

Why frustration again repeals its stand. Take the problem to the court who sits in judgment of your conscience. So heart carries the problem to conscience and they deliberate. Soul has to deliver the verdict and with this clear insight into affairs the ruffled and muffled frustration is ironed out all smooth.

Frustration begins when the living of each day is taken for granted. When this strange yarn begins to weave its own robe, the color becomes evident and the design apparent. Is the cloak of frustration because a need is existent? Is the yarn too heavy to carry the needle? Is the problem too bulky to finish the product? Is this garment of frustration woven out of materialism and wants? Or is this knitting a fine expression for the release of tension and the gift of creativity? Is the silver lining for the outfit all that's missing? While the yearning for the raiment becomes the obsession?

The outfit would be lovely for the wardrobe, but is it worth all the frustration to achieve it? Maybe today people think they have a need, when it's not the physical that needs protecting, but the inner lining of man that needs strengthening.

Journey Into Fulfillment, don't overload your vehicle with nonessentials. Take along the "must have's" without bending the springs. Take along the proud accomplishments within your heart and plan to enjoy this fabulous trip. Where meeting people is the lesson in learning and sharing the day's venture. Where sights form a new perspective and long ago frustration of the beginning is forgotten.

Why didn't we make this decision sooner? Let's travel now with lighter loads and lighter hearts. Frustration leaves when decision results and action becomes the actifying force in the course of events. Journey on with this milepost achieved and between here and the next great happiness is to enjoy.

Happiness is a state of mind and being, and place plays the background of events.

Face the word, fr/us/tr/ation/ as simply—
        (for us to give attenion).

Why, for us to give attention it all began, and now we're glad it was truly given!

III. AWAKENING TO AWARENESS

AUTUMN NOTES

A little hand carried crimson chrysanthemums to a somewhere out there teacher today. Sun caught a moment between grey blanketing clouds and brought beauty to the autumn hours. These notes of hurry seemed as tangible as the precious busy grey squirrel tribe pressed paws into action and nuts into hiding. Some secret hiding places are shared with this pen, and upon a winter day when the greys of nature meet, I'll feast these eyes upon his hidden treasure and this heart's sweet recollection.

Gardenia leaves all trimmed in wax are shadowing veined beauty beneath the gaze of sun. Like a velvet cloak of russet beauty a butterfly touched down to find a leafy resting place. The cloak was dressed like the chrysanthemum's crimson and God's great beauty had returned to re-vision.

Golden moments not at the foot of a far off rainbow, but great golden harmony noted upon this Autumn morning pressed into the notebook of Virginia Country. Dreams of an Albemarle countryside upon a photographed page of "Town & Country" and now heart seeks out this place.

Bursting golden happiness like Chapel chimes at dusk, this Autumn Day is welcomed by the sweet call of the songbirds, and enjoyed beside a window sill with fresh crisp morning reaching in. Autumn notes all shades today, up and down the scale of rhythm and melody. Great echoes to return upon a winter's day.

RESPONSIVE MEANING

To never leave such peaceful hours seems fulfillment's urging call. Journey laughs and nudges yearning like warm breezes in autumn's joy. The leaves of summer are changing hues and whisper crispy notes of praise.

Along this path toward the altar of reverence there dwell choirs to laud the hour and thought. People listen with intensity to the word captured between a harp of vibration and song. The two aisles walk across the ground of leaf coverlet and straight up to the entrance of message. The great sky above holding blue eternity, lines the cathedral of worship, while tree and limb are marked with prayer of litany and praise. Praises ring from silent hearts and listening awareness, this a camping sermon in the heart of Autumn's forest.

Meaning and purpose brought into closeness, while proximity of believers have congregated in unity. Journey Into Fulfillment the illusive moment when arrival has been attained. Attuning heart is matched in Soul's response and at last it is announced and leaps away.

Heart of Sunday in sunny havens now among life of memories. Rhythm of beauty and peace surrounding the day. Farewell to autumn and a paradise prepared, return the gesture with gracious adoration. Reach for another moment in capsuled happiness and journey continues with breath. Drink in these fulfilling times to feed the Soul upon another day.

WINGED EXPERIENCES

Just a little bit of maturity can sweep across the mind and bring decision into sharper focus.

Yellow chrysanthemum upon a wine-colored suit at its first college football game brings memories of courtship and youth. Tinges remain of that Homecoming Day when a first date became a lifetime beginning. Yellow chrysanthemum, the very largest kind, can pull the heart strings taut and the crimson wine wool can stir from a store window's allure.

Allurement of wishes to return one autumn day upon the wheel of life is Homecoming's triumphant march. Across the miles and from around the globe, footsteps return to an Alumni Reunion. For those who could not join in that great day's festivities it took wings of memories to bring it into their presence. What is stronger, the unity of memories of long ago and faraway places, or the reunion of people from faraway into proximity? Among memories there is no change except for dull trivia forgotten, and only the glowing recollections of faces and incidents retained. Handshakes clasp again in reunion, brings focus of memory and now into a sharp maturity, and contrast lies between the years having marched before.

Contrast in experiences makes lives each different and unique. The lines of time and maturity creases into the facial and becomes those genuinely happy, while harshness marks those less than their goals. Great numbers watch the parade of the college set today, and laugh at their own amusing antics of live opossums in dorms, and icy roofs for flag exchanges. Marathons to the Chicago Relays and Conferences across the States. Athletics so memorable when the stars all shared a common glory. Friends, among many, stranger but to a few, yet years upon the wheel how far you have moved?

Maturity turns the clock and counts away the experiences, while journey continues on. Fulfillment for a moment when journey brought the memories into actuality and the people all were gathered to glimpse maturity and a taste of success. A luncheon spread so fine and the fine cloth of years upon the table now. The silver array upon a strand or temple to give maturity a small distinguishing design. The plates are filled with happiness in sharing a reunion with friends. Memory will never remember the cost of the plate or that which was eaten. Satisfy memory better with a rare moment when fed with presence of friends and renewal of friendships.

The day too short for lasting, too short for saving, but one that remains forever best upon an Autumn Homecoming. Treasures of life to encompass in memory, truly this is a winged experience and Journey Fulfilled.

COUNTRY KITCHEN

There's absolutely nothing that could be more appealing upon a winter day than a country kitchen. Country kitchen could have any size, place, setting, and background. The aroma of country cooking and a warmed house has a fragrance like a bit of childhood happiness. Memories can be ignited upon a very tiny spark like kindling beside a wood burning stove. The grand old house that sends out a kitchen's invitation by the elements upon the stove. It doesn't take a cook all surrounded in finery to extend a welcome. Happy smiles and arms of greeting makes family hurry to the table of home for blessings and food.

There's a warm November sun smiling through the tall window frame. There's an oven with apples baking and special stew simmering upon the pale yellow electric stove. It's a gleaming clear day when blue skies reach into infinity and country cooking rushes there too.

There are no Shenandoah mountains in the picture window vertically placed but skies over the Chesapeake build snowy castles in haste. The churning river is out today to remind the country kitchen of butter upon an Ohio, Friday's wooden churn. All once upon a time. When little tiny pats were made with design in a butter mold. When the churn was washed in heated water from a stove and cooled so gently in water from a hand pump flowing. A pantry filled with pans, perhaps of artifacts today, and goodies canned by love and hand. Ruffled curtains ran up that long window rising too and a tiny river led past the gaze in the valley just below.

The willows would be shining upon this November Day and the gravel road would stop to cross the now metal bridge. The gravel road would walk on and climb a hill now running on, cross a larger bridge of Jerome Fork and on to church it lead.

There too a country kitchen but cold except upon special occasions. The road stopped and then turned around and came right back home to country kitchen living. Up from the recollections and into this Virginia setting — country kitchen here in the midst of a growing city. How can town and country be the same except in the eyes of the beholder? Journey forward and backward, just as nostalgic as the aroma upon the electric stove.

FINGERS OF FOG

Fingers of fog as nimble as a squirrel's leap. As quick as the wink of an eye and the wild call of nature, fog will dip down and cover both land and sound. The horns of fog toll out at sea and closer in a chime or two. Frosty fur upon a squirrel's tail matches this morning, and chills upon the spine as dampness creeps in. Tugboats call and harbors so near, all moving slowly as fog in the density cloaks more deeply. Porch lights dim but squirrels can find their winter treasures among the now dampened leaves across the ground. Fingers of fog seem to stop in a stance before skipping up a tree, limb, leaf and disappear.

Birds call to chatter, if it might be spring or fall, but squirrels assure it's the latter. Busy morning scampering between world and heart, no matter the size, no matter the season. Lawns alive with squirrels and fog, while a paper's crinkle ceases their hunt and nails upon the trunk sound just the same. So hurried the squirrel that collision with a cardinal out for its morning share, came as a surprise to both of nature's own. One so colorful not to miss, but fog and hurry discerned not their position. Crush of the gravel beside the river has tones of hesitation mixed with fog and chill. Fingers of fog crept in close, as unexpectedly as company and dishes upon the counter.

The squirrels chime their voices that none the matter, be it fog or other weather. On with the hunt, the nuts won't wait nor winter just beyond the fog.

So on with the dishes, sweeping and all, it's Monday when fingers of fog must carry on the day. Lift of the heart, lift of the fog, lift of the work and we might never have met on this threshold if it had not been for Fingers of Fog and another Autumn horn.

SIX O'CLOCK CHIMES

World at our doorstep, crossing the sky, cloaking out the church chimes at six. The tonight of winter has closed the door to chill and cold until a familiar sound must be let in. "Fount of every blessing," peals away the day and causes the listener to pause and reflect. The light of day has crossed the sky on its continual circuit. The darkness of night signals all to rest, but for the blessed few who hear the chimes above the evening noises. There's refreshment and pure security in sensing God's Hand that vibrates throughout the all of life.

Silent chimes rest until they toll another evening to close. The kitchen door stands still in waiting to be closed and keep the warmth in, and the world out. Sweet evening of quiet unmapped and here. Time for listening to voices surrounding the heart of home. Time now to be glad all are safe within the fold of home. Few find the peace of this hour, for dishes glare to be washed, a shirt looks bland before its starch, a shoe is dull until shined. A play to write before the Christmas season has settled closer.

There's a doorstep of thought upon the threshold of evening and the screen allows its entrance. The steps were steady the day is spent and now to close it like the chilling door. Farther away, another church chimes, unheard until tonight. The crispness of winter brings the tones across the river, untouched by leaves that have gone away. Another chime is tolling the day to close too, and chill repeats its chilly note.

Silence of six o'clock evening and freshness of air from near the sea. Oceans of happiness in depths uncounted, until stopped and surveyed in the veiling close. Blessed assurance, happiness dwells not outside the screen or on the doorstep, but right within the heart that journeys into silence and listens to the beat of living that has given so much. Master of Heaven who grants it in daily blessings, and dwells in heart's retreat.

The warmth inside makes the difference.

EDGE OF DECISION

Upon the edge of decision bare feet touch sensitive rug The nap beneath is suddenly softer, or coarser dependent upon the edge of positive or negative emotion. Sensitivity to wishes woven into reality, yet keener yet the desire of "Thy Will Be Done." Upon the throne of evening come eager plans with enthusiastic heart. Visiting friends from near and far, returning to reunite in short hours of meeting. Edge of decision could change all that, but prayers raised upon many days at closing, "God Bless All of Our Family and Friends" wherever they are, brings this prayer to encompass a moment of those and time. The edge of decision of expectant change hinges upon anticipation and unknown the direction. Life upon the move, and many doors have been a short time key to enter, live and leave. What part of world, what part of life, will next decision choose to become?

Edge of decision, wearing softer like the pencil with thought. Where goes this hour, where goes this day, from the eternal of its purpose? Edge of decision moves closer and yet has found intuition prepared, mind alerted, heart in perpetual beat, and lips with the answer, "Here am I!" Here are we and there we were.

Life of challenge, filled to its brim, alive with meaning, and the pathway visible upon the step. Where from here, but ready be, where but soon, the days will dispatch. Hour of vigil upon edge of the new, hour of hope upon the threshold of light, and hour of night before the dawn. Edge of decision, without a backward glance, it is part of the free choice and thread that unwinds upon the spool of daily living. Contentment yields and edge of decision becomes a new plateau of living and journey unfolds.

CHIFFON EFFECT

Without a moment to glance away a chiffon profile upon coiffure brought a strange analogy. Dressed in rose sweater, beige skirt, and brown, brown shoes and hosiery to match the shading. A long conversation caught the profile in hidden scarf effect. The beauty salon receptionist was helpful in phone calls for the lady, maybe calling a cab, or helpful for a sitter and the talk goes on. Today's intimate dialog with people is seldom experienced by time allotments and why this one? When why hit my eye, and searching for the answer, it was hidden beyond the black veil. The chiffon scarf gave Afro's illusion and all skin to match, seemed this part of makeup and totality. So studying a moment the black scarf turned and beneath its neatly tied triangular corners came a madonna's face as sweet as nature's own provision. The time was given for she was genuine, and unknowing in her choice of garb to give another view.

How often do we appear before others' eyes so different from what the mirror reflects to us? Our own image is in full view of others and profiles too give a partial effect. What others see is the personality and individuality, while our own self consciousness looks just for the style. "How do I look" a question before entering upon a special scene? Or powder room mirror, for catching a head to toe glimpse, but veils still are visible when genuineness is hidden.

Move farther away and perspective seems wider, the features may be less significant but the figure of people still pass in and out of sight. Look for the sights that seldom are seen by the illusions created by actions. The silver white hose to create another desire, when Creator of All fashioned the greatest cosmetic case of color upon this planet. Au naturel with sparkling eyes, gleaming hair for crowns to be, a mouth to express from the inner out, the mind to embrace a depth of kingdom given and held within. Hands to work and mind to inneract, while feet to move, across this stage. Actors none could compete for a trophy of greater value, than to be found with greater talents beyond the script.

Does the veil hide the potential of each, or have to be found, a "self" created for higher destiny? Veil of life, withholds reality.

IV. INNER TRACES OF URGING

HEART'S CONCERTO

Concerto of the heart, a beat of rhythm that's enduring, priceless and resoundingly memorable.

This masterpiece came into reality by realization that each life is a composer of greatness. The many lives crisscrossing makes for friendships that build from youth, maturity and on toward eternity. Great marches have been composed by the cadence of step into mastery upon the printed line. Music of symphonies chorusing through this mansion of heart seems lifting toward heaven in resonance. The depth of peace is punctuated by happiness trills and scales like a stairstep going upward.

Realizations may be upon the very edge of a linen thread, recognized upon the dining room table, while clearing the empty plates and chairs to neatness. The beauty of time around the table in fellowship and it lingers long after all have sought another page of the concerto of day.

The little dust and crumbs upon the carpet seem to float and not leave heart heavy with work thoughts to remove. The sunshine beams through sheer layers of folds, delight and appreciation. Children's voices above splashing merriment, home where all will again return like lyrics of a chorus being repeated with continued harmony. Melody of this day, play louder for mind to grasp with eternal reconciliation to the Master's Plan for entity and Heaven. Orchestra in tune to the greatest director, mankind yet strives for this unity of purpose, and the blending of efforts into the greatest peace ever composed.

Blue sky above takes the melodies higher, and Apollo 12 emits a dream into higher destination. How high this man, when moon he has soared, how high the mind when soars it beyond into infinity of its creation?

Concerto of heart is the surging tempo of goals beyond those seen by yet human eye. The radiating depth of soul reaching out for expression and being met with vibrations of the greatest composition ever written. Words and notes seem to peal deeper and only penetration of silence could hear them all.

ART OF THE CONCERNED

Journey Into Fulfillment is not a guaranteed passport for the unconcerned. It is however, the art of traversing life with awareness for seeking more than what mediocrity offers.

Clouds of doubt and concerned thought will mark the path and when beauty breaks through in brilliance, then sensitivity must be attuned to what a small ray of light might mean.

Purpose of concern, and analysis of question may result in a giant step forward by an individual yet benefit more than his own concept discerned. Clearance at an underpass guarantees the distance from surface to surface, what does concerned thought offer? Does it challenge the path like a tunnel to traverse?

Values written and ideological in scope will offer a scale toward reaching goals. Ladders of success climbed by the score yet height to each may be measured only by the degree of growth, "from beginning to goal."

CIRCLETS OF INSPIRATION

The swirling, whirling, last leaves of Autumn are caught in breath of wind and funneled in circlets from ground to sky. The leafy exchange from limb to ground seems to beckon the spirits of man to watch his own whirl wind of life in a fleeting second. The golden droplets lose shape in the myriad dance before the gaze of noonday sun. Driving through these pictures of mystery, makes self glad to be alive, and eyes to reach the summits in appreciation.

Life of many whirl in a blurr of existence, while from isles of Greece to shores of continents to visit, there are those who do believe in the "Honey Years."

From clasps of leaves leaving a trail to follow, and small veined jewelry beneath a step, to Operation Handclasp on its written way to another's heart. Journey of nature and journey of man, each cycles onward in lift and fall. Rise of the Spirit into reach of Soul, like empathy of freedom by the flying leaves. Leaf upon the ground now crushed, raked and burned, all these little temporals disappear to make room for the new buds of maturity in wisdom. Where have all the leaves gone, back to rest upon the carpet of earth, lifted high in heaven's breezes, cloaking now earth's beauty. Limbs of heaven soaring on with growth, budding, becoming and forever within the eye of man's own Soul. *Vision for perception, Soul for penetration and Heaven for the totality of perfection.*

Reaching moment by moment for the betterness of man, is living by example, and journeying farther into the seconds, hours, days and years of purpose. Leaves for the seconds, branches for the days, trees for the seasons, and life in dwelling for the years. Eternity within, and Heaven joining its company, while winds of today are a fragment of both.

Life how beautiful in its heritage, and breath how cherished by its living force, and Soul the key to greater treasure. Sensitivity built with yearning for depth and gained in quiet dedication, while all knowledge flows in endless panorama of the Living Presence.

HALF-TIME

Gnats rising in formation like planes before their target. Their little aerial maneuvers search for the landing without the touch of orders from ground control. The little ships at dusk floating in their mooring signals, are the hundreds of wild ducks reaching quiet shores for rest. Like little clucking chickens discussing the situation, while sharper calls are mallard's own trumpet.

Walk along the sandy shores just before the dusk and in this civilized living a tiny nook hears only ducklings call, waters splashing and the night breezes from the ocean clinging. Mirrored trees rise up from this rivertide and reach further than the tranquil branches of day could touch. The swamp grass is burnished in bronze and heavy gold tones like whiskers of the day growing longer at the night's return.

The horizon draws closer and lights reach out in welcoming splendor, upon the threshold of evening and quiet. The warmth of day has gone, while inside the great oyster colored house music rings in concert and footsteps upon stairsteps linger in echo. Thanksgiving, for the minute things that eyes often do not appreciate, in the hurried motion of their choices.

Lower the threshold of continual work, slow the sweep of the empire of thought and learn the beauty of a cozy moment. When does Soul dial its own discovery and bring fresh alertness — is it at low tide or in high tide of experiences?

Does the current daily clicking become the life's highlights in a fast colosseum of spectators, or does aloneness find its own meditative seat? No charge for a ticket on life's greatest half-time, between the scrimmage and the touch down. Where are you now?

THE NATURAL EFFECT

The glittering attempts to lure the eye are even succeeding past the pornographic strata into the once sheltered home's magazine subscriptions. Subscribe and within a period the ads take on a new shape, or filmy see through in its attempt to raise its sales. The natural in the flesh seems to have even reached the Sunday Morning news edition and it's flung out across the lawn by a hurried delivery. The world can't be shut out and isolation is not our lot, but recognizing why it's now on our doorstep is vital and can be indicative of our understanding of others and self.

Children may find it stimulating and this must be reached within the realm of choosing, the good and bad, in what we are continually exposed. The expose is their admission that even the new couturier styles aren't giving them the real freedom they are trying to self style.

The reality of it is Soul can't be released by the material disrobing, and to those that seek this media upon the publicized fig leaf still haven't met self in the mirror. The natural effect is their searching for that inner desire to be open to new philosophy in thought, and discarding the old material forms of cover-up stereotypes. The clothing in this writer's opinion often exudes the inner person's frustrating "face-not" the outer makeup, the hairdo, as most see as the only personality.

The natural effect will actually become the inner response when the hopes, and fears are recognized by each one, and a new being is produced from within, containing the humanity and compassion that Christ's own cross brought to light.

Natural form of tree and thought, should reach its highest potential by becoming honest, sensitive and positive in recognition of Christ's presence and God's fulfilling purpose. Examine your own thought motives, and crumble not, in that as clay dries it must be moistened and remolded in a worthy form. Sunlight has faded, new lights come on — wherefore who lights your inner self — you the created, or God the Creator? By the Creator the created has room to grow and natural form is in view of moral perfection.

ONE-HALF A PAIR

After the glitter, sparkle and lights are gone, and a short dose of sleep has been administered, the party is over, and all languages say, "Good morning!" The band played on and on, with some of the old recognizable tunes and steps. The people gay in their very own way. The International Set with ribbons and medals for men and laces with bows for their ladies attending. This holiday of lights and color swayed, rolled thick like pastries in foreign accents, and the world was small beneath the styrofoam snowflakes reaching toward the great billowing parachute clouds above. Gold balloons hung within circles, swayed and seemed like solar systems that are.

The party is over and a silver glove missing but thoughts of a beautiful experience go undampened away. Holidays around the world seemed to bring a spirit of people in authority away from the seriousness and for a brief hour a world of smiles and this was their own communication. Saturday's formal is hanging so still, and Sunday's awakening is approaching us all. The beauty of Sunday written in the morning sounds and already in motion beyond the window.

In only a few hours, the Christmas pageantry is about to begin when angels dress and make their entrance. When choirs climb up to their heavenly, lofty seats. While cherubs sing and fidget away, and the director breathes a last small prayer of hope. The lights dim again, and spotlights focus, and glitter and color, sparkle and all rises again from physical realms to heavenly portrayals. "When Angels Speak" a title with a yearning, while the play speaks on to those who have come.

I'll carry my left silver glove in a purse that's hidden in knowing that in the right hand is God's own silvery one. The pair is complete because man in all his attempts can never do it all, a touch of the Master's Hand must always surround. One right glove missing from last night's party. Would we ever like to think that God would be the finder? Who would have invited Him to that Saturday Holiday flare? Do you go where He wouldn't be hurt by your presence there?

We took Christ to the party last night with friends who are Christian and shared our table. We talked of tithes, and the Second Coming, who would have known of our quiet talk amidst the band and gay voices? Tired the body of physical man, who labors on or parties too long, the energy of quiet in these meditative moments, tie yesterday and today into a pair, but the wisdom of the pageant must yet be witnessed. Lift us onward and in the right hand of God there is no missing glove. A purpose to have only half a pair, when silver, gold, and lights are only part of it.

There's a comet coming, A Star of Bethlehem again!
Is your whole life relevant or is there still a glove missing?

V. THE PHYSICAL REMINDERS OF VALUE

A PACKAGE OF ATTIC THOUGHTS

One box covered with dust from uncirculated thought bears this paragraph of an heirloom. "Preserving the remnants of an era passing, when Old World and New mingled, jelled and now the jam of memories is beyond the care of this generation between the farewell and the acquiring." Another recollection of a sight in motion but now so still "The chestnut coursers raced the land ahead of wind and sun. The upturned faces of leaves in flight seemed gentle."

When the visit of faraway people changed from distance to proximity, this paragraph reached out to express itself. "Islands and mainlands touch not by land mass visible, but connected by waters pounding and flights recurring." Friends in lands faraway meet upon shores of unexpected encounter and though years have separated, the same distinctiveness remains. Stature upward, can be recognized by the carriage of the person which memory recalls. Thus visits of the Caribbean fly into today's experience, renew the memory, and move away in return.

In the attic there is quietude of the boxes of possessions, opened and sealed. Like thoughts, some contents are personal, valuable and some worthless. How orderly is our attic of quiet thought, or doesn't it have a small light to illuminate? No matter the boxes, it's important that special moments have opportunity to be packaged and saved, and worthy of every move that ever was decreed.

Wrap these in the ageless ribbon of recall, dry them gently in the cell of memory, and save only the timeless heirlooms of respect. "Attic Thoughts" are no longer lost scraps of living, they are collected, saved and loved.

TRANQUILITY BASE

Tranquility base on neighbor moon became reality in A.D. reckoning. The probing into the solar systems from early man to modern man, in his reaching out attempt to find a dimension of inner answer, to where is wholeness? No moon walk this personal footing, but its name was more nearly true for man was in transit from earth to moon, to touch the theretofore untouched sphere and in quietness must have found tranquility. To live in a State, one of our fifty, found a small segment steeped in history, reaching toward the modern look, along the route of time to heal the wounds of a civil strife. There in that State, unlike the majority— life was less complex in hectic pace, and achieving toward a balance in peace, tranquility and progression not stagnation. The time clock of a verdict changed this scene and now amid these hearts lies turmoil, a race with time, and a desperation of longing for their former tranquility. No system has perfection in earthly eyes, but to destroy all that has been— to make room for change, leaves chaos and destruction at the heartline base of society and individuality lies behind the doors where families live.

Tranquility base like society desire, yet criteria for achievement must reckon with, impact of history, heritage and the leavening of time. Across the Father of Rivers, in a land of high-tempered humidity, let winter's cooling winds bring a more tranquil hope to save the spark of rebellion from igniting. Tran-quility or guilty?

THAT WHICH IS WITHIN

The Spirit within man is like a knife forgotten and frozen in remaining cake. When the need arises the knife is found, allowed to warm and its cutting edge becomes useable.

The Spirit within seeks great expression yet like the pencil new, as long as it is not sharpened the pencil is unuseable. Find the Spirit within is like man's feeble search and running to and fro. It doesn't happen in the frantic moments, it comes in knowing there's an undying need for more than physical food. Spiritual food responds like enlightenment to the Soul, and awakes the depth of man to longed for expression beyond his own meager intelligence. When these moments arrive, if the pace of living allows this moment to capture this depth of growth, then the small voice within is heard by Soul, pulsating its message into a vibrating concept, thought or motive.

Journey Into Fulfillment, is this hand-in-hand search to unite daily living with Spiritual awareness, and produce a magnetic meaning to this earthly existence between heaven and return. This in-between can well be the hell on earth, if the Spirit is never loosened from its icy bondage of man's untouched heart. The cake has thawed, the knife warmed, both have served their desserts.

INSTEAD

The red-headed woodpecker with a little brown tie, is out tattooing her way across the world. Her lunch was awaiting a hasty peck, while my sandwich dried watching these wintry newcomers. Cardinal and shadow just flew aloft, from playing in raindrops drawing circles. He's hunched on a limb with time to judge, sharpen his beak and be gone in a wink. A cheery song of Christmas in a "Pear Tree," seems perfectly logical on its wintry limbs, as adorned it is by the colors of its winged and feathery friends.

The misty rains of December with a tinge of Spring arousing, is like packages beneath an evergreen, but "Do Not Open." It's a grey Persian day when snoozing is inviting, but baking a pumpkin pie brings a spicy dessert instead. It's a day when frosting won't frost, and instant pudding won't gelatin, when letters to be written were ignored instead. That funny kind of day when lazy thoughts reach an ebb, or relax and enjoy the day. To read a book instead of write one, to sew instead of mend, to play a game instead of iron, to skip directions instead of follow. To leave the crumbs upon the plate, instead of rinse and dry, caress the dust instead of the cloth, and watch out the window in daydream thoughts instead of televisions applaud. To dream a picture instead of brush it free, to listen to the raindrops beat instead of a stereo's many speakers chant.

Instead, seems the title and gentle its mortar, for to "hurry" would burst the quiet, and to "forget" would erase the peace. The timer on pies declares its finish and the rheostat rises and today is ever present, but now sensitive and lovely like the bonsai pine which isn't mine.

VI. MENTAL INTO SPIRIT AND RETURN

EXPERIMENTING WITH EXPRESSION

How do attitudes and thoughts become tangible expressions? There are so many qualities of these mentally stimulating attributes. The level of development can be readily accessible by the inner desire for its coming into central concentration.

Let's try poinsettias? I love this flower plant that grows in fields along the Southern California shores of the Pacific. From the artificial arrangement upon the table their presence recalls the natural environment in which I have experienced real living plants. From fields of red poinsettias to those as tall as the old Spanish hacienda that has protected these tall but fragile creations. The soft casaba yellow like a rare melon, these poinsettias too attract the eye. When leaves fall and the stalks stand like giant bending canes, but all lighted with those red pointed leaves — these are poinsettias.

They are like the holly berries and mistletoe that make the holidays burst into a floral arrangement. As its clinging vines cluster amidst tree branches and seem to dare any climber to set them free, it is mistletoe: alive and blowing high in the winds. They are up so high like giant woven baskets with white berries abounding, like tiny pearls so far from the sea.

The short thought began with simply the instruments of paper and pen. Finding a peaceful nook, is an enjoyable sight to stimulate a former experience into new written expression.

A special little tool that helps to carve out the artificial and make it a reality is a small but forceful instrument of prayer. Today I asked "Please Dear God — help me to express the beauty of the poinsettia in the window!" So small a prayer, but the communication of openness was all that was required. How much more alive and dynamic our lives would be if we but asked, "Dear God help me to..." The openness to God's nearness brings great dimension into living, new energy into our weary physical beings, and fields of gently flowing thoughts upon the shorelines of peace.

The little artificial poinsettia in the driftwood vase hasn't changed. It is still only a replica of the real, but the prayerful thought of expressing its presence has unfolded more than all of its petals upturned.

Beauty comes in seeking, and release comes in expressing. Beholding and believing changes the artificial into the real — how genuine are we every day?

SERENADE OF CHRISTMAS THOUGHTS

Silent Night, all the lights have lost their glare. The candles surrounding the Holy Creche lift the shadows, and angels seem to be singing of heavenly peace. Still night around the sleeping hemisphere — The Star of Bethlehem bursts into the heavens and the heavenly light for civilizations now and yet to come, to see and to believe. The long-awaited Messiah is being drawn to earthly life by God's Power and man's hope. Stillness so beautiful, silence so golden, and candles so caressing in tender light. Christmas music swells into the air and hearts are changed by the moment of grace, beauty and peace.

Clouds nod and bow and soft flakes of snow come gently to rest. The glistening night of Stars and Snow quilt the earth in a pure blanket of a clean new day of hope having come to life. Freshly fallen snow reminds man of his need for cleansing and the Messiah will show the way. A small baby to grow in God's image, and His Wisdom and to be the Almighty Son of God, who came to lift man from his lowly step. What a glorious gift for God's created man to have available, within reach, and within comprehension.

Christ the babe, grew and became the living symbol of peace, protection and friend to all men of believing heart.

THE LONG DRY SPELL

The long drought of ceasing to express the inner promptings into tangible recognition is the long dry spell. When the summer of heat refuses to give forth the rains of refreshing need, then the farmer too speaks of the long dry spell, in hopes of a miracle to release the elements and produce drops of moisture for his fields to grow.

Listening now in the winter's cold chill, there comes soft drops against the window like the answer heard from a farmer's plea. The sunshine and droplets radiate a glistening effect and the long dry spell of expression is quenched, like the dry throat searching for moisture too. The long dry spell has had time for thought, time for new goals, and time for growth between the planting and the harvest.

Man and his growth seldom breaks noticeably from one growth ring into the next, like the growth rings within the tree to count its aging years. Man's growth is a blending of thought and personality into a maturity of action that is tempered by experience and time. The long dry spell may come when least expected or anticipated, but must be respected for its timely entrance and that which becomes a result of productivity.

When blue skies up above, which seem to offer the heights to challenge, and the sun to encourage. Then the dryness of living has been quenched by the determination to forge ahead, and where else would our lives ever realize the difference between miracles and nothingless? Small droplets rest and evaporate, small thoughts burst forth and without recognition also become vapor lost and time forgotten. The long dry spell heeded, remembered and withdrawn.

VIDEO MIND

Mind, an object of human development. Mind, a storehouse of whatever man has experienced. The brain is a sensitive mechanism, mechanical in the voluntary or involuntary surges of response. The brain sends impulses throughout the body through mind's network of fine electrical vibrations. The brain is the organ, but mind is that which lives forever.

Regardless of the educational development of the mind the property of recall is in some degree existent. With continual operational reflection, mind becomes the atoning force in which (the atonement) with God can be judged. Judgment by God of man's life is a continual vibrating instrument — leading man toward the next stage in his positive development. The degree of man in the beginning of his sensitive awareness to God within, God surround, and God speaking. Throughout this mind — waves of thought are on a permanent invisible tape — like a tape recorder, and the footage marked by events and time in living.

Looking back in reflection to relive a moment is not a new consideration, but filed in memory's keeping. But to close the eyes, and visualize a person with only the name for the implementing, and thinking of this person brings a degree of closeness of communication more fragile than a written letter, but video mind is satisfied. Sound and thought, of mind's lock and combination — to the "safe of security" within, is invisible to the human touch, but relevant to that which makes life filled with greater dimension.

So conscience upon an experience can judge the mind and the more positive the living the less negative is found shadowing this life. Life, is man's own dimension, toward the expressive element that is visible.

Video mind is one of the most creative engineering forces that the Creator has given Man. People, places, time, is like a great personal Smithsonian in recording, and Video Mind in positive psychological tune is a march of the Soul toward perfection.

FULL MEASURE OF SATISFACTION

Full measure of satisfaction is not like the hot cup of tea — it's a feeling that has been reached through expression and meaning. It comes for a man when a great accomplishment has been attained, a small core of worth has excelled and a moment of satisfaction encountered. Or it may come for him at the polish of a shoe or a car's gleaming shine, but all an effort given by choice, and not from any demanding of service. Full measure of satisfaction is a completeness of best and the price of time goes untagged.

This same full measure of satisfaction may come for a woman upon completion of a deed, given in time, effort and love. Like a present just completed from hem to zipper and buttons that match the garment, now it's finished, pressed, packaged and ready for its surprise opening. The full measure came at completion and the joy of its owner will never be seen from across the mountainous miles but a child's joy reaches the heights and is a satisfaction in knowledge. Full measure — so quiet in its entrance and exit, yet for a brief second the flashing joy was received and is sent along to another. Like the Spirit of Christmas that lingers after the tree is gone and the candles unlit, the moments of sharing, with peace and happiness abounding, these are the priceless treasures of full measure. The satisfaction is the realization that the joy was made whole in its inner quiet moment.

There's time for everything, and a season too, but little time given to remember the full measure upon the cup of blessings poured out by the Infinite Power of all Life. We Thank Thee, for this second of completeness in sharing with others the small service given.

TURN AHEAD

This road ends and where to from here? Sometimes the thought — sometimes the sign, "No turn space, or dead end ahead." The road of Route 1969 from Interstate and on, this road ending and a new route ahead. Follow the directions, or live it by the instinctive, no one can answer, but just between yourself and the thoughts.

The year now ending, so quiet it's fading, only the wind to howl its closing, and only a sigh for its signature. The new year ahead in so short the time, like a new year to live and like a baby that will grow from infant of a day into child of 365 days. The clock knows no answer to this event of change, and only man and his fine dreams can behold the setting. Farewell a year filled with sights and heights of great beauty, farewell the years of greater striving and caring marked by each person who dared to take that turn in the road. *Happiness* comes along from this year into the new, as the fuel for warmth when the spark is so fragile. *Love* carries on from each year to another if it's treasured and cherished as those for whom it is given.

Accomplishments have gained the roadway access too, and these make the new highway ahead firm, strong and a foundation upon which to continue. *Health* is brought too, in a special case of gratitude, used and returned in filling energy as the outpouring is granted. *Knowledge* is granted a visa to travel this highway too, and a finer instrument to be engineered as it is used, tuned and perfected. *Sight and insight* were given a green light and the bridge between darkness of day and soul was not suspended.

Gifts of the spirit the most fragile of the parcels, were given a moment to be renewed and in hopes of greater using upon this continuing roadway of life. Thoughts, dreams and goals are a heart and mind's reward for careful using, retaining and for building. A life was the key for the ignition and travel, a life now more dedicated becomes the magnetic course upon which the new year can begin.

Life how precious — yet fleeting as the seconds, beautiful as the created spark, and a temple of strange colors and shapes. Architecture of life, as intricate as a bridge, yet from the structure to the heights it's only as strong as its depths and heights in balance. Life in tune, life in focus, life in balance with the greater scales suspended by the linking of God's presence.

A new year to encounter, and a new year to build. May it be filled with the blessings of God's own protective Hand. Turn of the clock, turn of the page, and into your life comes the greatest *turn!*

VII. THE HIGH ROAD

BLANK FOR BEGINNING

Drawing a blank card on any game played is like losing a turn as the other players move ahead. A blank in a shell is the container without its explosive element. A blank paper seems empty and unpromising and yet the complete beauty of the untouched is inviting to be used. All these blanks seem empty, lacking and unproductive. Yet the absorbing of stillness, the release of worries, yes the blank is like emptying the frustrations and allowing a new beginning.

For what is each individual hunting with the equipment of surrounding life? What game is being played before your eyes? Are you participating or only the shell without its implementing enthusiasm? Could lives be as blank as the fresh new paper before its use? Yes! Taking time for the most important lifts life into a fresh reality. Doing the things that are a growing experience for you and others around you. Taking trivia and letting it lie until the vacuum sweeper catches it and dust in one breath.

Putting aside the demands that press and live a little of the moments of blessed demandlessness! This is not futility but a necessity for the composing of mind's mastery of living, the Soul's storehouse of strength and the Spirit's renewing fuel of caring. The inner caring, the inner bubbling of energy to differentiate the useful from the useless of each day!

Seasons know quiet and seasons prove growth, seasons produce harvest and seasons need rest. Man produces daily in his striving, seeks diligently for his workaday harvest, and only nightly short rest for renewal. There are seasons of rest and thought needed for each day, as well as the accomplishing satisfaction of day's productivity, but a moment to stop the treadmill of rolling wheels gives the body, mind and soul its readiness for the next start.

A moment uncharted for whatever the choice, is rare, and a blank moment when mind is uncluttered, heart open, body still, and spirit willing — it is the beginning of a journey in listening for the still small voice revealing a new realm of living and coming into the Presence of a new companion, whose name is Saviour and the blank then becomes filled with Peace. Journey Into Fulfillment can be a filling experience into renewing life.

JOURNEY'S THRONE

The position of the seat, whether forward or reclining gives the condition a relationship, but the elevation unmarked. Journey has a position of beginning and the seat of this travel may well float like an innertube with the tide and little thought. The seat may be lifted to a camel's difficult structure and jolt with the steps and the thoughts as disturbed. The seat in a vehicle of car rushing forward requires a seat belt for safety and a readjustment of your sights may occur. The airline seat will guarantee you the heights of its own pressurized permit, yet thought lifted, elevated and reaching perspective would well be worth the price. Travel, a way of movement, need not be fast, or slow, it can all be done upon the seat of arm chair and quiet. Throne without the "r" and substituting "e" can become "the one" and this is a position for meditation. Rest in the moment, whatever its position, lean upon the Almighty for the great strength and existing need.

Throne needs no place, seat needs no upholstery, it only needs the individual to recognize that Journey will accept any stature, size or ticket, but again it promises a vision of grandeur for all eyes if they choose, but no guarantee of enjoyment without the key to sensitivity being carried daily. Rush of this life past the thrones of work and challenge, but to the foot of only One Throne must the individual ever need complete recounting. Dare to journey toward a far country with vision and hope is a fulfillment in recognizing beginning.

Sweep of the eye, hand and thought is like the velvet fabric of a fragile throne, Higher, yet Higher, climb to the stars, all this in search of the continued path toward ultimate fulfillment in God's tender care. Throne no physical boundary for sitting now — but the carpet of Journey, beckons onward in its direction.

THE FILTERING SILENCE

Dear Lord touch the arm that yields the pen that flows across the line. Dear Lord touch the heart that enfolded a thought from some hidden throb. Touch the ears that discern the audible, and let the song of soul harmonize the whole.

Thoughts that cascade like waterfalls of summer seem to stand still in winter's touch. Snowflakes swirling in their own wintry heaven, break through the pulse of play and fall like broken stars. The ground drinks their luster in a moment of thirst and not until the quenching has passed into a frozen state do they again cluster into their own comfort of perfection. Journey Into Fulfillment has spun like a wheel of great desire toward a yearned-for attainment, and now at last with the first snow of winter's picture — the scene seems completed, a coverlet to protect, the warmth that has grown within.

Journey has climbed to the summits of hope, swirled with the hesitation of man, lifted with the Hand of Spirits change, and come to rest as all in time must accept. Fulfillment, a search that Journey has reached toward, and "Into" each heart a little meaning of life penetrated. Journey leaves your company for the narrow road ahead of your own footsteps in search of the Spirit of personal infilling power, and Holy Spirit's flame to light the path. Alone never, and to rest an assurance of peace within the fulfillment. Journey how precious the trail this vision has found, and fulfillment of renewed faith to also move forward. Journey Into Fulfillment in silence we rest.

ALTAR OF ENCOUNTER

To prepare to come before the altar of God has a manifold significance. First comes the removal of the dry dead limbs of our own surface being. Down past that layer of superficiality like the skin's own protection. Down through the layers of awareness, but yet no penetrating sensitivity. Into the tunnels where sounds distract, into the strata where soul reaches spirit's wave.

So like the floral arrangement of dormant apple branches prepared with the dripping white glue, and sprinkle of glitter, arranged into an eye of pleasing symmetry, and a white poinsettia's face lifting up in silent admiration. One branch became broken for want of space to reach out, this lower branch symbolizing man, and the taller three the Trinity all perfect. The feeling from the artist's touch broke through the artificial and into inner delight. Prepared for the altar of a Sunday worship, yet the unknown fever of illness brought the arrangement into the home where the worship must also become the heart of the family and man's growth too. Daily preparedness for meeting face to face upon the last altar to give — life, and in its retreating measures it must have left the artificial, glue and glitter behind.

Movement into a perfection of man's potential proclaimed by Christ will grant fulfillment for the instant, a promise of returning peace when prepared to encounter again another measure of blessings given. The breakthrough is so available with recognition of the power of Christ's fellowship within life. Journey need not be with constant motion, it can be perceived with the Quietude of souls expression, and neither words or directions can be read here by the eyes of man, it must come from darkness into light, and man moving from the artificial broken life into the uplifting quest for higher purpose, souls fulfillment upon the altar man's spirit prepared. Readiness for direction of how physical life is to be lived. Moving from element to element within the laboratory is explainable, but little is defined as presence meeting Presence, and spirit meeting Spirit.

Altar of encounter, reaching heights beyond the apple branches, and no cup will ever hold the measure of blessings that will abound. Abundance in living lives within the dormant winter, and promises bursting growth with the signal of a new season in new found fulfillment.

Journey never ceases, fulfillment always in the refilling waters promised by Jesus for thirst, and life the element in which this journey moves on.

PRAISE TO LIFT

To praise is to lift the worth of, mankind to a goal higher, to raise the vision toward greater destiny. Reaching the darkness of dejection can find only light from above. And to raise the eyes and see the praises not for the ego growth but the soul's own carol of need to be filled, and fulfilled — this is to be lifted by care, value and need.

Let the eyes not waver upon the path toward the goal — nor the heart falter for the fear of height — nor the lungs of physical become as without air for the vital force to continue. Destination is a pinnacle if the journey has reached out, aided and lifted the giver and receiver. So this too is praise in the production of value — worth, of an intangible creative need for encouragement. In our age men need this bit of praise by encouragement to strive for the best within, and the best in return.

THE PERFECT SIGNATURE

A winter feeling steals across the silent world at rest. The great quilt falling comes quickly to its appointed scene. The beautiful untracked print of winter's soft kiss is pressing down against the sleeping branches, the touseled grass that needs some miracle of beauty. The restless tide bears the new touch with a song of silent rhythm while a smile crosses the river and the flakes become the river's frosty breath exclaiming welcome. All homes are freshly dressed in a white winter robe, and the clouds are lost in the whirling winter world of gusty and hasty adieu.

The doors of home close tighter with the screen of summer gone, here is honeycomb winter—by winter's brush. The sidewalk all cracked is now smooth and perfect in this fresh hour of snow's return. The darkened house now begins to rest in slumber, comforted by today that's spent, night that bids, and tomorrow in its silent footsteps approaching.

This heart a living song, races up and on. The light of day slipped early away, the light of man is dimmed in an instant, while the light of soul remains within—in an aura of mystery of how it's retained, yet kindles brighter with the miracle of awaited experience. Light of the Creator, granted unto the created and found to be the greatest energy of invisible force—Rise Up and He Did!

Falling snow, the beauty of a perfect signature—GOD!

CONTENTMENT'S FORM

Contentment is a feeling that the masses are hard set to procure. Neither capsule or a turned on feeling in the phobia of our pushbutton society can assure contentment. The searching for peace in its inner dimensions of man's being is like a maze entangled with noise crisscrossing the confusion diverting the intent.

High above in the evening dusk a familiar noise purrs through the sky. The shape of this contentment is the pilot at the stick and his view is enlarged and magnificent in the evening altitude and magnitude of his own comprehension.

The rigidity of life's schedules does not find often time for spontaneous expression. In the quiet house, a child finds that finishing a new book with the welcomed scent of mince pie is just the piece of relaxing that a young form of ten can enjoy on a winter evening. A teen finds great mountains of books in a scholarly world of term papers to be a noble seclusion and yet a security in the outline and purpose. So reading once a tool has become like a magnetic course that is a natural contentment in its beholder.

The river beyond was hidden by summer's cape of green, and yet today it bends its arms just the same. An enduring picture in its own boundary for the hour.

Peace returns as simply as putting life back into its ordered recognition of God and His Universe holding plan in perfect balance. A tiny portion perhaps in the genetic cells that has been bequeathed to each entity and this is God within, and peace in a sensitive form neither in mist or fog, or sunlight can it be touched. Contentment is a quality of the inner self's own personal realization.

TRY TO RETIRE

Trying to retire from the vocational race takes planning and years ahead in readying. Learning a hobby is the prescription on the contract, but enjoying its expression of the real you, must be a well chosen hobby. Subject re-tire, is like the car that needs new shoes, don't use retreads on this journey. A lifetime of work means the best was given of energy and time, and traveling now needs new tires for best friction. Changing the tire and changing the pace of living is a symbol of beginning another facet to living. Back to the hobby! Don't say television is going to be my only channel change activity. The hobby must be an inner and outer expression of the zest you have in reserve for these dynamic and exciting years.

Try to retire is taking a few moments everyday in the first learning to live with self and finding the individual you really are. This retirement contract isn't like buying a tract home and expecting every blueprint for living it to be the same. The floor plan for retirement has many closets, doors and individual dreams really custom made.

Retiring should be your own creative custom planned endeavor, planned structurally as an architect would dream. Laid together foundationally sound as a mason's skill, open and alive as the beautiful windows with the view you have chosen to live with.

Trying to retire is an exerted effort to be prepared for and here too comes an individual journey into life's fulfillment, just as each day can be the very best. Putting all the dreams for tomorrow into a packet and in the safety deposit box, is paying rent on the box of contents without any light for growing. Investing time in planning is a responsibility to yourself even at 20-30-40, that's not the policy that can wait for maturity — it's a thinking ahead of how each day can be a joy, and trying to retire will be the key to everyday not to one day when the contract expires.

Retire can mean a little rest — for the prefix (re means beginning) and a new journey it will be.

ENTERING IN

To enter in means the entrance into a place, situation or atmosphere. To those who yearn for quiet rest there is a place. To those who seek the powerful Presence there must be an atmosphere of willingness. And to those who seek for the Spirit to yield greater fruits then there must be preparedness of situation. To each there is an "entering in" and within this moment of stillness as the fresh new morning, there comes peace from the pressures of the "pick up and clean up work a day world." Lifting of the physical pressures, because awareness of greater things lie hidden within the wave lengths of indwelling communication with God.

Prayer upon the lips is the act of bringing physical into a willful act and the mind and heart demonstrating its expression. Silent prayer upon the stillness has brought physical and mental together in a meeting of spiritual endeavor. The seeking of Divine Wisdom as an instrument of learning the Divine Will is like the untouched frost of a new morning. The beauty and perfection is glistening, refreshing and brings untold dimension of uplift to the entire being. Entering in must become so much a part of living that its need is as evident as breathing in and out for the lungs. The Presence of Spirit is ever surrounding but the totality of awareness is rarely given by man's daily thrust toward living.

The pollution of air, skies, and water is only a part of the environment encroached upon by many feverish wills for the place called success. The life is so demanding for constant recognition of "self" and when "self finds this still— is not satisfaction in the ultimate — then Journey Into Fulfillment can begin."

The road of "entering in" is an entrance of "yield" first of desire of flesh, and merge into the stream of heavenly plan. Exit by the toll gate is a normal freeway habit, but exit from the higher place is as quick as a sound, the flash of a thought and the closing of a door. No one is forced to enter or leave, but the returning for peace becomes the entering in needed for daily lift. The "coming out" is for the living of better lives in witness of the Journey In and Out. God's Presence is forever the radiance as illumination of place, and for path.

THE GREAT QUEST!

Why is conversing with God so hard to find the time? Why is reaching out so intangibly difficult to extend? Why is man so unapproachable, by fleeting attitude and disappearing conscience?

The night was, and rest the intended departure, from the circuits of thought and physical activity. The night awoke, and amid a city where country does not touch came the rooster's crow. Listen again the sound must be wrong. And the crowing was, and sleep was not. Why so early, like a silent creeping cat, why had it crept away?

God speaks in the every waking, sleeping breath of man, but in deeper silence of man's nature the impenetrable is accessible. Seeking out the why and how, He is speaking, when the conversation is like with a man who cannot hear, but only see; and God who hears and sees but speaks in a silent language of penetrating sensitivity. The vibrations are different and the clue is in the awareness to these differences.

God guides the fate and destiny in His all pervailing eye, yet man's own choice can free the experience and dash away. In questing for the Divine Will the requesting must be within the heart, the surrounding events will guide and direct these fragile paths — if eyes are eager, ears are sensitive, and heart is willing. Mind is so moveable, changeable and transient in its tuning, it must be guided, and returned like a high frequency in its channeling. Wisdom is forever abounding the lives of all the created, but the Divine Will must be selected and continually absorbed or else it is diverted and never lost, but usually unnoticed.

Conversing with the most powerful force in existence is a lifting high above the physical sleeping or dosing existence and in a constant desiring to also be creating. Creating and expressing what is unseen, unheard, but allowed to flow by this instrument called "man" — each of us is capable of being all the pens and brushes of the great Almighty Creator in His expressing.

How sensitive is man? How ultimate is man's potential? Have we reached out beyond the last limb of grasp and found new foundations of strength and purpose? Dawn rises, the cock crows again — who can sleep while mysteries await the unfolding? A train whistle signals a crossing, wheels rumble upon a track and the veil closes. The exhilaration of the morning has brought new energy, but *peace* has erased the questioning and the *quest* has been fulfilling.

Journey Into Fulfillment we have met again!

GOD'S MEANING AND AUTHOR'S INSPIRATION

Life that's so full and rich, so much to do — so much to give — what shall I do first? Time so short it blows away while a tune is hummed, but gathered in the folds there is a warm glow of happiness. Life is so full of experiences that meet again in friendship renewed, years of becoming and so much to do because of the growing. Life is full and richly abundant in blessings, so much to respond in thankful ways. How shall the mind of man pursue it all and do it well? An answer comes in Proverbs so true to this — "The mind of man has many plans, but the purpose of God is established."

So much to do, life is so full, what to choose and here is the best answer. Doing the purpose of the established plan of God for man and within this purpose encompasses the physical workings of the daily life and then there is time. Time for peace and time to grow, time to become and time to be filled. Journey Into Fulfillment will continue for each Soul until all that God has purposed has been fulfilled.

Journey Into Fulfillment will forever move the mind, and soul of man in challenge of the purpose to be fulfilled.

No ending for us to write but until the last word has been proclaimed by God for man.

JOURNEY INTO FULFILLMENT BREATHES ON IN YOU.

FUNDERBURG LIBRARY
MANCHESTER COLLEGE
Gift
of
Cdr. & Mrs. Dan M. Shafer

WITHDRAWN
from
Funderburg Library